RYAN NEWELL

I0135894

Dark Psychology and Persuasion

Understand The World Of Dark Psychology With All The Techniques Of Manipulation And Mind Control

Table of Content

Introduction

I t is the study of the human condition because it involves people's psychological nature; that is, they prey on other people with criminal activities and criminal motives. Illegal reasons and unlawful purposes lack instinct and social science theories. All human beings may harm other humans and creatures. Although many people have suppressed or sublimated this trend, some have acted on these impulses. Dark psychology attempts to understand the thoughts, feelings, perceptions, and subjective processing systems that lead to predatory behavior contrary to the contemporary understanding of human behavior. Dark psychology assumes that crime, deviance, and abuse are purposeful and have rational, goal-oriented motivation 99.99% of the time. It is the remaining 0.01% of the dark psychology part of Adler's theory and teleology. Dark psychology assumes an area in the human mind that enables some people to perform cruel behavior without a purpose. In this theory, it is called a dark singularity.

Dark psychology believes that all humanity's malicious intentions towards others vary from minimal ambiguous and short thoughts to purely psychotic deviant behavior, without any rationality of cohesion. That is called a dark continuum. Dark psychology calls it the confounding factor. The mitigating factor is the promoter and attractant close to the mysterious singularity. The heinous behavior of people falls on the dark continuum. A brief introduction to these concepts is as follows. Dark psychology is a concept that the author has struggled with for fifteen years. It was only recently that he finally conceptualized the human condition, philosophy, and psychology definition. Dark psychology covers all the people who connect us to the dark side. All cultures, all faiths, and all humanity suffer from this well-known cancer. From the moment we are born to our death, there is a latent side within us, which some people call evil. In contrast, others define it as crime, immorality, and pathology.

Dark Psychology introduces a third philosophical construction, arguing that these behaviors are different from religious teachings and contemporary social science theories. Dark psychology believes that some people will act the same, not for power, money, gender, retribution, or any other known purpose. They commit these terrible acts without aim. Simply put, their use does not justify their methods. Some people assault and hurt others because of this. There is this potential in all of us. The area the author explores may be to harm others for no reason, no explanation, or purposelessness. Dark psychology believes that this dark potential is very complicated and even confusing to define. Dark psychology assumes that we all have the potential for predator behavior and that this potential can enter our thoughts, feelings, and perceptions. As you will read through this manual, we all have this potential, but only a few of us will make a difference. All of us once had the thought and feeling of acting cruelly. All of us have thought about hurting others seriously and without mercy.

You are honest with yourself. You have to agree with the thoughts and feelings you once thought about committing heinous behavior. Given this fact, we consider ourselves to be a kind species. We want to believe that these thoughts and feelings do not exist. Unfortunately, we all have these ideas, and fortunately, no action has taken against them. Dark psychology constitutes that some people have the same thoughts, feelings, and opinions but act deliberately or impulsively. The apparent difference is that they operate independently, while others only have brief thoughts and feelings about it. "Dark Psychology" believes that this predator style is purposeful and has a specific rational, goal-oriented motivation. Religion, philosophy, psychology, and other dogmas have made convincing attempts to define dark psychology. Most human behaviors related to evil practices are indeed purposeful and goal-oriented. Still, dark psychology believes that persistent behavior and goal-oriented motives seem to be blurred in a particular field.

From thought to pure psychosis, dark psychology has suffered continuous damage without any apparent rationality or purpose. This continuum, the dark continuum, helps conceptualize the philosophy of dark psychology. Dark psychology addresses human psychology or the general human condition that allows or might even promote predatory behavior. In many cases, this behavioral tendency's specific characteristics lack the rational motivation of universality and predictability. Dark psychology believes that this general human condition is different or an extension of evolution. Let's look at some basic principles of development. First of all, consider that we have evolved from other animals. At present, we are a model of all animal life. Our frontal lobe makes us apex creatures. Now let us suppose that being advanced creatures does not entirely separate us from animals' instincts and predatory nature.

Chapter 1. What Is Dark Psychology?

T he idea of psychology is to help people by helping them understand themselves. Dark psychology is about using the mental weaknesses that people have to get people to do what you want them to do. I know it sounds cringe worth to many people, but this is not nearly as bad as you think it is. The fact is that everywhere around, the tools of dark psychology are chipping away at your mind. Facebook ran a test on its users by curating their content and measuring their mood. They wanted to see how showing people more negative content would affect their news by showing them more positive content. Magazines and advertisements like to play on your need to keep up with the Joneses or not lose something. In doing so, you are drawn into whatever they are selling. The news feeds a looping heap of controlled opinions to try and make you agree with the viewpoint you already share. The world is full of psychology being used darkly, and most of the time, you are on the receiving end of it rather than getting the benefit of it.

That is about to change. Dark Psychology is about recognizing the compulsions, needs, and desires that we all have, which can be used to get what we want.

What Do We Mean by That?

Whether it is a fear of loss, a desire to keep up with the Joneses, or a need to feel wanted or feel right, these things guide our decisions and impulses, whether we like them or not.

Alternatively, whether we want them to or not, people act against their interests every day simply because they are in an emotional state that guides your actions. When someone finds out these emotional triggers, it is a matter of time before they can start to guide your actions, control your behavior, and even manipulate you.

There can be nothing worse when people have figured out your emotional triggers and begin to play them. Whether it is a parent or a stranger, you can feel yourself often taking action and not even certain why you feel drawn to taking action just knowing that you have to, or want to, or that it is something that must be done. No, you cannot wait and Dark Psychology is the tool that sets this into action. It is the tool that shines a light on finding all these mental triggers in yourself and others.

It also recognizes that as amazing as our brains are, they take many shortcuts in the name of efficiency, which leaves them vulnerable to some of the simplest attacks. Ideally, our minds should not make us feel sad simply because we had a negative thought, and yet, this happens all the time. We're wandering around, having a good time, a good day. Someone says something or does something, maybe even inconsequential, and yet suddenly, our mood is shifted, and we have to fight to get back to balance. Our brains, however, are just working to be efficient; they are not working to be perfect. And when you understand that, you know that there is a huge opportunity to be had when dealing with people. More importantly, you understand that there are something's that you need to learn to safeguard yourself.

You have desires and wants, needs, and how far you are willing to go to have those things met. Do you know? What are your buying triggers? What are your emotional triggers? You have them, but are you completely aware of them. What makes you stressed, confused, angry, happy, and excited? All of these things are inside your mind? They are inside everyone's mind. When you know how to access them, you will suddenly have greater freedom, happiness, excitement, and possibility in yourself and others. Because finally, you will be bringing your desires to life by getting others to see and want to help.

We are going to address manipulation—one of the keys to dark psychology. Manipulation is different from persuasion, influence, sales, and other such things. It is often about getting people to take action by playing on their weaknesses. We will talk about the ethics of manipulation, what you need to think about, and the "Right now" is essential to set the stage for what you can expect and learn the handful of psychological techniques and methods that will allow you to control people.

Dark Psychology is a tool, like a hammer. You can use it to build things or use it as a weapon to hurt people. We are making no moral judgments and go about using these skills. But the most important thing is for you to learn these techniques to make sure that you have a better understanding of yourself and what people are using against you.

The world can be a dangerous place knowing these techniques and understanding how people can manipulate you or fundamentally transform how you respond to people and how you engage with them. You will recognize when people are trying to use your emotional states and trying to take advantage of you. You will also learn how to use these techniques in ethical ways so that you can guide people to take the best action for themselves or the action you think they should take. Beyond everything, you will discover through the dark psychology what exactly is triggering your behaviors and, in part two, how to change those triggers if they are not going to be helpful or serve you in the way that you want them to.

Dark Psychology involves the use of mind tricks, which is in between deception and persuasion. The psychological mind tricks might sound outrageous, but it works well. They are being used to mislead people to think that what they know to be right is wrong, and what they believe to be wrong is right.

In a simple term, dark psychology allows humans to be willing and deliberate to harm others through their decisions and actions; sometimes, this might not be physical. However, some emotions are groomed from a very early stage of an individual's life. For example, a child grows to learn how to cry so that the adults around will make themselves available for their bidding. We can call this crying a manipulative tool for the child to be enabled to control people around. As a child grows up, if such as a child is not being cautioned on what he's doing, the so-called innocent childish behavior would now become a dark way of controlling people to do what he/she wants.

Dark psychology is the study of how a person thinks and sees a need to understand the intent behind actions and words. In general, it illuminates the dark side of human nature. In dark psychology, the effect is experienced by both the victim and the perpetrator. The personality traits which are considered as dark include narcissism, psychopathy, and Machiavellianism.

In a simple term, an excessive admiration of oneself in an obsessive manner towards appearance is referred to as narcissism. Narcissists usually feel superior. They do not subscribe to the rule of giving and take in a normal relationship. They are good at blaming others whenever there is an issue. A common feature is to be an extremely self-centered individual. Narcissists have a public appetite for control and power. They control people by making them think that they are looking out for them. They are also very smart such that they get involved in your day to day activities in life without being noticed. Above all, they are Keen liars and master is the lie skills.

Psychopathy is a trait that is associated with not being sensitive to other people. A psychopath will almost not have empathy for other people. Psychopaths are usually bold, confident, and fearless. They are risk-takers and extremely charming.

On the other hand, the third personality trait is known as Machiavelli's; the term is used to describe someone who lacks emotions and desire to achieve something at the expense of other people's feelings. This can be done through deceit, manipulation, or going against some moral rules. An individual who scores highly in Machiavelli's test is usually referred to as a "High Mach." These people are always around us, sometimes in our workplace or as a neighbor. They are hard-working people who are smart and are unapologetic about stepping on other people's toe. This set of people are opportunists and can emotionally detach themselves from situations they are in. Due to this ability, they are capable of involving themselves in several sexual several encounters. They can stand a chance of being good teammates but certainly not a good friend.

This knowledge of dark psychology is to protect yourself from those personalities when you come across them. Dark psychology cuts across all human conditions in which are universal. It studies how the state of humans relates to their thoughts, feelings, and perception. The general assumption here is that every human has the potential to be violent. Learning this concept is of two-folded benefits. First, it helps individuals accept that they tend to become evil, so the knowledge of this will prevent it from erupting. And secondly, it gives everyone a reason to struggle to survive.

The following concept I will be talking about is Neuro-Linguistics Programming (NLP). This is a technique used in restructuring people's minds on how to get rid of bad habits, how to become productive, and how to make them effective in general. You can use this technique to connect sense, mind, behavior, and language. This method is designed so that you tend to control people without them even being aware of what you are doing to them.

Neuro refers to the nervous system, which is made up of the mind and all other senses. Your nervous system functions when you interact with your environment or people. That's why when you listen more to people, you get to understand what is being said. When you pay more attention to what happens around you, you know and see more things about people around you.

Chapter 2. Explication of Dark Psychology

S everal skills are essential in analyzing people. The first and perhaps most important skill is having an understanding of human nature and normal human behavior. If you do not understand how humans behave under normal circumstances or what motivates most people, you are unlikely to interpret others' actions and intentions correctly. Just as a judge relies on their sense of how people typically behave and what motivates them in their judgments, so too must you develop an understanding of the typical spectrum of human behavior to analyze someone properly.

Of course, human beings can behave in highly original ways, making analyzing them difficult at times. Although human beings frequently behave in typically human ways–like being jealous of others' success or envious of a colleague who just married a beautiful wife–sometimes people can surprise you. Indeed, some people never feel jealous or envious of others. Most poor people do not steal even though they may need this because it is not part of their character. Frequently the most significant, most flamboyant thief is the person who already has all that they need.

To analyze people, you are going to have to start with knowing how humans are generally. It includes understanding the spectrum of human emotion, the behaviors linked to these emotions, and the things that motivate people to do this. Everyone wears a mask, which means that sometimes the intentions of others are not always clear. But even with this mask, people can reveal their emotional state to you, the things that make them happy, and the things that make them sad.

We all wear a mask, but perhaps only FBI agents are so skilled that they never give you some clue. A spontaneous laugh, a twinkle in the eye, a giddy tapping of the foot: These are unconscious signs that men and women give of how they feel. Analyzing men and women will require understanding human behavior and interpreting what people say and do.

Non-Verbal Communication

Non-verbal communication refers to the little clues that others give us that convey essential information outside of language. Human beings are social animals, meaning we evolved in settings where we were generally close to one another rather than alone. For this reason, we developed the ability to perceive and interpret the signals that others send to indicate their emotional state, thoughts, and motivations.

It is easy to pay attention to words when we are attempting to analyze others. Still, because language is not always an accurate indication of how people feel, it is essential to pay attention to the non-verbal cues others send. These cues can include facial expression, body distance, and the position of hands, quick movements of the hands or the feet, and the like. These non-verbal cues are not specific to human beings. Non-human primates are excellent examples of how animal societies can be built without speech. From bearing of teeth to the tail position, apes have a language comprised entirely of non-verbal cues.

Differentiating Fake From Real Emotion

Analyzing others will require developing the ability to distinguish exact sentiment from a false one. Human beings know that others observe and interpret them, at least the intelligent ones do, so they have become adept at hiding their feelings. A typical example of this is someone who smiles even though they are not happy. Still, this hiding of emotion can mean angry when one is hurt or vulnerable. Human beings wear masks to protect themselves, as you must if you plan on defending yourself from practitioners of dark psychology. But protecting yourself also means analyzing people appropriately, and this means determining which emotions are real and which are not.

The practitioner of dark psychological tactics perceives you as prey, so they pay very close attention to your words, actions, and non-verbal cues: virtually anything that indicates what's going on inside. You may put a wall to make your emotions more difficult for the predator to access, but you will most likely say or do something to reveal the truth. This is just as true of the predator as it is of you, the prey. They can put on a façade of smiles and pleasantries, but sometimes all it takes is one fierce look to reveal that their intentions are not so friendly.

We see this all the time in films and television shows. The new neighbor seems nice, but the camera shot reveals their subtle change in expression when your back is turned. They are not so neighborly. Their goal is to steal your husband and wreak havoc in your life (in the case of the standard Lifetime Original Movie). To protect yourself, you need to use your understanding of human nature and analyze it to figure out what is going on. Is there a discrepancy between the surface emotion and the events taking place? Perhaps the other person is smiling, but you heard that they lost their house and are short of funds. Would most people be so giddy in this situation?

An essential part of distinguishing real from fake emotion is deciding whether the surface or "fake" feeling makes sense, given what you know. Human beings are good at being emotionally aware by dint of being so communal. A person can hide what they feel, but it may only take a brief glimmer of real emotion for you to establish the rule of what is real in this person and what is not. The other person drops their mask for a second and notes what the natural person beneath looks like.

Tips to Identify a Liar

Anyone who has spent time around a pathological liar knows that little tricks can be used to tell when fibbing. Pathological liars are often highly friendly people who love to talk and always have something to say. It is this still having something to say that gets them into trouble. If you are suspicious that the person you are speaking to is a pathological liar, pay attention to the factual aspects of the things they say. This will become natural in time as you become aware the person is lying. You will make a mental note about facts like a specific monetary amount of something, a date, or a restaurant's name because you know these things may potentially be false.

Paying close attention to the details is the first step in identifying a liar. The second is knowing when to face the liar with the facts. It may not be a good idea to confront them pointedly, as you may decide. If they said they went to a particular restaurant, ask them what they had to eat—baked chicken and mixed vegetable stir fry. The next day, s/he asks them how the steak was. If they say, it was beautiful when you have caught them. They did not go to the restaurant at all. A pathological liar tells so many lies that they cannot keep track of them.

Chapter 3. How To Use Dark Psychology

How Can Psychology Improve Your Life?

T he following are some of the top ten realistic uses for psychology in regular life:

1. Get Prompted

Whether your purpose is to stop smoking, lose weight, or examine a new language, psychology training provides pointers for buying motivation. To grow your motivation while drawing close to a project, make use of some of the following tips derived from research in cognitive and educational psychology:

- Introduce new or novel factors to hold your interest high.

- Vary the series to help stave off boredom.

- Study new matters that build on your present understanding.

- Set clear goals that might be at once related to the assignment.

2. Enhance Your Management Abilities

It doesn't count number in case you're an office supervisor or a volunteer at a neighborhood teenage activity group; having true leadership abilities will, in all likelihood, be vital sometime in the future for your existence. Now, not all of us are born leaders, but some easy suggestions from mental studies can improve your leadership capabilities.

One of the most famous research papers on this topic looked at three distinct management styles. Primarily based on the findings of this look at and subsequent studies, practice several of the following when you are in a management function:

- Offer clear steering but permit group contributors to voice opinions.

- Communicate approximately possible answers to troubles with contributors to the group.

- Focus on stimulating ideas and be inclined to praise creativity.

3. Come to be a Better Communicator

Conversation involves a whole lot more than just the way you speak or write. Research indicates that nonverbal indicators make up a big portion of our interpersonal communications

Some key strategies encompass the subsequent:

- Use proper eye contact.

- Start noticing nonverbal indicators in others.

- Learn to use your tone of voice to boost your message.

4. Learn To Better Understand Others

Just like nonverbal communication, your capacity to apprehend your emotions and the feelings of those around you perform an important role in your relationships and professional lifestyles. The time emotional intelligence refers to your potential to apprehend each of your emotions in addition to those of other human beings.

What can you do to emerge as more emotionally stable? Recall a few of the subsequent techniques:

- Cautiously assess your very own emotional reactions.

- Record your enjoyment and emotions in a journal.

- Try to see situations from the angle of a different person.

5. Make Extra Correct Selections

Studies in cognitive psychology supply a wealth of statistics about choice making. By making use of those techniques for your lifestyles, you can discover ways to make wiser choices. The following time you want to make a huge decision, strive the usage of several the subsequent techniques:

- Try using the "Six Thinking Hats" technique with the aid of searching on the situation from multiple points of view, including rational, emotional, intuitive, creative, advantageous, and Dark views.

- Recall the capacity prices and blessings of choice.

- Appoint a grid evaluation approach that offers a score for how a selected decision will fulfill unique requirements you may have.

6. Enhance Your Reminiscence

Have you ever wondered why you can remember the precise information of childhood events yet forget the call of the new customer you met yesterday? Research on how we form new reminiscences and how and why we forget has caused some of the findings that can be implemented without delay in your daily life.

What are some methods you can grow your reminiscence of electricity?

- Awareness of the data.

- Rehearse what you have discovered.

- Do away with distractions.

7. Make Wiser financial decisions

Nobel Prize-winning psychologist Daniel Kahneman and his colleague Amos Tversky performed a chain of research that looked at how humans manipulate uncertainty and danger while making decisions.

One looks at located that workers could extra than triple their financial savings by making use of some of the following strategies:

- Don't procrastinate. Start investing savings now.

- Commit earlier to dedicate quantities of your future profits to your retirement financial savings.

- Try to be aware of non-public biases that may result in Dark money choices.

8. Get Higher Grades

The subsequent time you are tempted to whine about pop quizzes, midterms, or finals, consider that research has confirmed that taking checks helps you better consider what you have learned, even if it wasn't on the test.

Every other study discovered that repeated check-taking might be a higher reminiscence aid than studying. College students who were tested repeatedly have been able to remember 61% of the content while looking at the group recalled the most effective 40%. How can you observe those findings to your lifestyles? While seeking to research new data, self-check frequently to cement what you have learned into your memory.

9. Become More Effective

Occasionally, it looks as if there are hundreds of books, blogs, and magazine articles telling us the way to get more completed in an afternoon. However, how much of this advice is based on real studies? For example, think about the variety of times you have ever heard that multitasking can help you become more productive. Studies have discovered that trying to carry out multiple missions at the same time severely impairs pace, accuracy, and productiveness.

What classes from psychology can you operate to boom your productivity? Consider several of the following:

- Avoid multitasking while running on complex or dangerous obligations.

- Cognizance at the venture at hand.

- Eliminate distractions.

10. Be Healthier

Psychology also can be a useful device for improving your ordinary health. From approaches to encourage workout and better nutrients to new remedies for melancholy, the sector of fitness psychology gives a wealth of beneficial strategies that can help you to be more healthy and happier.

Some examples that you may practice at once in your very own existence:

- Research has shown that both daylight and synthetic mild can reduce the symptoms of seasonal affective sickness.

- Studies have demonstrated that exercise can contribute to more mental well-being.

- Studies have determined that supporting people apprehend the dangers of bad behaviors can lead to healthier choices.

Chapter 4. Delving Into Dark Psychology

S ome of the best science fiction that has ever been written has surrounded the subject of mind control and its ability to control our world. However, it can still sound like a futuristic event. However, many neuroscientists are continuing to create a digital interface specifically designed to connect to the brain, which has continued to make progress in recent times. Even though this advanced technology is still unreachable, it has made plenty of headway where we could see mind control gadgets popping up everywhere shortly.

Currently, a technology known as brain-computer interfaces, or BCIs, has only been in the development stage for individuals who have fallen victim to injuries, debilitating such as being paralyzed. A great example of this is a paraplegic by the name of Dennis DeGray. Neuroscientists at Stanford University assisted DeGray in creating a major breakthrough and a typing world record involving mind control.

DeGray's success partially stems from the assistance of Jaimie Henderson. Henderson, a neurosurgeon at Stanford, successfully implanted two electrodes arrays the size of a tic-tac into DeGray's brain. DeGray's brain activity is then monitored by the electrode arrays, which helps decode electrical brain signals that neurons fire deep in the brain's motor cortex. The results achieved were beyond impressive and allowed for the early steps of achieving independence for many currently fully or partially paralyzed people. With a lot of interest pointed towards this ability to control the environment through a BCI, many researchers hope that future demonstrations can further the technology in the future ahead. It could even be as soon as the next 5-10 years that we could see more of it being integrated into people's lives.

Besides the research and development being conducted at Stanford, another company seems to be taking it one step further. Neural ink, founded by Tesla and SpaceX CEO Elon Musk, has become dedicated to creating BCI that they have labeled as "neural lace." To date, Neuralink has already raised close to $30 million for funding the project.

Nevertheless, like anything connected to the internet, one has to be extremely careful and diligent in the security and safe handling of all devices so that the device's security does not become compromised. We saw this occur when the Mirai botnet practically destroyed many internet areas that created attacks that used Denial of Service. Once a person's brain is implanted and connected to an internet device, this is when an entirely new level of security issues could occur, including a possible 'brain jacking.' Not only for security purposes, but it also could lead to many questions about ethical responsibility. For example, if a brain-controlled machine breaks the law, then who is arrested for it? Problems like this would need to require in-depth discussion before our future becomes a place where mind control is used for everything. However, in the short-term, an interface that is a less invasive brain-computer is already in use and which have significantly lower risks.

Many headsets have been developed and used in many drone races successfully as well as controlling Mind Desktop, which is a brain interface that is generalized for the use of Windows. With these devices, they bring less of a risk than implanting a chip into your brain. Not only that, but they do lack a few things too, especially with performance. This is seen with Mind Desktop, where a character is typed in 20 seconds. Regardless of that, they are still pretty cheap because of their use of electronics that have been modified. Therefore, if you currently have Mind Desktop, you are using an $800 "electroencephalogram" (a medical device used to measure brain activity) for a fraction of the real machine's cost.

When it comes to external BCI challenges, they mostly surround the skull, brain coverings, and scalps density and thickness. These characteristics prevent us from snooping on the brain's neurons with accuracy, which is what we think is essential for a BCI system to be high performing. As far as the future is concerned, we can only get remotely close to the information found on neurons is if we get an implant placed inside.

With many researchers making attempts to build a better BCI, other researchers have continued with their BCI implant technology. However, they have been experiencing technical issues of their own, which they will need to overcome. First, they hope to obtain an increased amount of views from their sensors, which will increase their ability to decode faster brain signals a lot more accurately. Plus, there remains the question of getting these outsides of the laboratory so people can use them.

These BCI's need to be constructed not to require a technician or some third-party intervention is of high importance since the main goal includes restoring people's independence while being paralyzed. This is why researchers are continuing to address these issues actively.

The erasing and implanting of memories seem to be only capable in movies such as Total Recall, Dark City, and Inception. But this idea no longer sounds as farfetched as we once thought since many people do not even lose sleep over the fact that it could happen someday. But now we can begin to see a brighter future with ontogenetic and how it continues to tamper with memory to bring it to light eventually. Although ontogenetic is still a relatively new procedure in the experimental stage, it has broken some laboratory ground. It uses light to activate or inactivate neurons that are highly specific by way of light-sensitive channels. For these to be used, they also require sensitive proteins. A few of these proteins include halorhodopsin or channelrhodopsin, which are added to the subject. These proteins are found naturally in many organisms. They need to be inserted genetically into an organism like in a rat or mice in the laboratory. Once injected, the neuron will fire every time the light is activated. When the light is on, the light enacts discretionary particles' progression, such as calcium or sodium, making the neuron produce an activity potential.

This system has been utilized in mice to control their eating or drinking propensities. The mice are hereditarily built to have these light-touchy proteins, and a wire is embedded into their cerebrum. Specialists demonstrated that the mice would keep eating while the light is turned on, regardless of whether they do not feel hungry. The best way to prevent the mice from eating is by killing the light. By basically turning on or off a light, one can control a neuron from terminating, bringing about certain and automatic conduct changes. This procedure can be utilized to figure out which neurons are required for specific activities. Likewise, researchers would now be able to figure out what capacity a neuron has by initiating it or deactivating and watching the impacts.

There have been a few speculations that caffeine may avert memory deficiencies by restraining the adenosine A2A receptor. A recent report demonstrated that the actuation of adenosine A2A receptor in the hippocampus, utilizing ontogenetic, was sufficient to weaken spatial memory in mice. This investigation not just exhibits the relationship between caffeine and abatement in memory misfortune; however, this additionally demonstrates the likelihood of erasing and hindering recollections in mice utilizing ontogenetic. Another investigation demonstrated that if neurons in the thalamic core reunions were initiated utilizing ontogenetic, the working memory in mice indicated deficiencies. As this system turns out to be further developed and used, researchers will frequently have a superior comprehension of which neurons influence memory and how they influence it.

Ontogenetic was utilized to take a gander at the impact of core cucumbers (NAC) on the "cocaine-setting related" memory guideline. They found that when the NAC neurons were enacted, the mice basically "overlooked" that cocaine was situated in that district. The researcher likewise saw that the actuation caused a diminished number of c-Fos+ cells in the VP, which has recently been related to a "decline in medication chasing." They presumed that these neurons were significant for the directing prize looking for conduct brought about by cocaine. This might be significant for deciding how a habit is shaped and maybe helping expansion issues.

This demonstrates the significance of certain natural triggers for medication addicts. If ontogenetic can help cancel the recollections engaged with the situations, it can have exceptional consequences for how we treat chronic drug habits. Not exclusively would memories be able to be deleted, yet false recollections can likewise be included. A recent report demonstrated that when dentate gyrus neurons were enacted, mice solidified in a spot where they had never been stunned, indicating dread. This dread was not there earlier, yet after the light was demonstrated, these mice had recollections of dread in a novel spot.

Even though ontogenetic is genuinely new, it is rapidly being consolidated into numerous tests. It is enabling us to all the more likely comprehend what impact enacting or deactivating neurons has on conduct. Unmistakably it is conceivable, at any rate in mice, to cause a mouse to do certain things utilizing optogenetics; we can even eradicate recollections and "make" new ones. One day those science fiction films may not look so inconceivable.

I do not mean the enthusiastic control intentionally used to get our particular manner. I mean the capacity to get others to figure out how we do and concur with us, just by the sheer quality of psyche.

Consider despots who can bewilder hordes of individuals with quality of speech while on the ascent to control. Analyze the content sometime in the not too distant future. You think it is difficult to see in what capacity numerous individuals moved toward becoming influenced around then. Consider a well-prepared canine or horse and the association with their proprietor. A steed is more grounded than the proprietor, and a canine normally increasingly deft, yet they obey directions. Consider the impact of "charm." How does a specific entertainer hold a crowd of people while similar words or activities by another entertainer are less captivating?

Are these things the aftereffect of the idea structure billows of extraordinary power, created by a solitary individual who empties their feelings into the conveyance and into that idea structure cloud? Rather than a few contemplations, social events to cause a solid cloud can include a solitary individual who has excellent conviction and self-conviction blended with crude feeling produce their cloud that overwhelms the psyches in the crowd?

In most close to home connections, there are fluctuating degrees of control, some favoring one individual one minute and the other the following minute. Equalization is accomplished at the point when intense feeling bolsters amazing personalities.

Chapter 5. The History of Dark Psychology

H uman mythology is riddled with tales of ghosts and creatures that behave in such drastic ways. The very description sends chills down the adults' length that listened to such stories as relayed by past musicians and bards. The creation of monsters advises us that perhaps the universe is not as secure as it might seem from within our window. Beasts live among us and render our lifestyles as something to be protected against, as anything to be covered.

Maybe a creature crawls out of the closet while you rest in your room or slips in from a backdoor that you failed to lock. Perhaps you assumed you were over there, but as it enters your door, you listen to footprints crackling upstairs and a soft voice roaring. You see a bushy, tail-like foot poking out beneath the bed or a claw. You notice a massive, vicious laugh while running for life. You sprint into the shower, and the door is locked. It's not necessarily a stellar exit strategy as there is no window in your toilet, but you didn't know where to get off. Maybe the beast is on the escalators. You don't know where everything is. But after that, you push the above head bathroom light chain and see that you are the monster.

Monsters exist among humans and are medically related to as H. Sapiens... sapiens. Aliens from some other world did not commit actions of murder, theft, and ruin. They were living things who decided to commit these crimes, and today they also live among us. There is indeed a term in behavioral genetics, the so-called dark chord. Applies to the three characteristics of psychopathy, narcissism, and sociopathy, such as factors are deemed especially harmful, so distinguishing such people from the general public is necessary, or would it be?

Since ancient times, an argument could be made that human beings accept their character's horrific components. Today we believe in everyday practices of ancient history, such as orgiastic religious practices, human sacrifice, and ritualized murder as brutal acts of the past that indicate a better forgotten time. Still, it has been argued that these acts represent social and cultural outlets for the black universe that lies beneath the beautiful surface of the human outside.

Societies were then explicitly organized. This would be up upon you to determine whether things are more comfortable today or bad. As tacky as the past, as mentioned earlier, practices may have been, their career status within their living area represented an acknowledgment. That human being had a wrong side to their personality. It was great to give outlets to this dark side than to let it explode and simmer in unexpected ways. For what do today's gang stalking, serial murder, cybercrime, and narcissistic and antisocial acts portray, but living things give in to ends of themselves because they have already expressed themselves in other ways?

The argument is not to assert that living things must consider to give in to their so-called dark tendency of singularity, but to recommend that the contemporary art of mind control represents a variety of activities expressed in ancient society in unique ways. Although the conversation of societies' tradition of providing into their character's dark sides may seem incidental to the discussion of mind control, few things could be essential. A significant phase in planning for defense lies in understanding anyone, you know, maybe the perpetrator of these black arts. It could be someone you already understand.

History of Dark Psychology Study

The 2 social scientific patterns that proactive solutions-day dark psychology are undoubtedly abnormal psychology and psychology for individuals. Irregular psychology is a psychology experiment concerned with psychological illness-related habits of behaviors, emotion, and behavior. These emotions, thoughts, and actions can precede a psychiatric disorder and are usually thought abnormal. As psychology tends to construct a relatively linear dichotomy between normal versus strange behavior, a sociological factor will come under the scepter between irregular or atypical behavioral forms instead of actions assumed to be inside the usual spectrum.

In the early late nineteenth century, person psychology was founded on human conduct driven by the purposeful activity compared to latent libido and sex impulses that describe Freudian psychoanalysis. While we have already addressed in some depth the degree to which individual acts are not consciously driven. May thus be viewed as non-purpose, person psychology allows for implicit or involuntary motives. It just appears to recognize them when non-Freudian, benevolent, and even not always implicit.

For example, as a motivating factor for action, Alfred Adler focused many of his texts on superiority complexes. He found that people who handled the situation in angry or otherwise unbecoming ways were generally inspired by a sense of inadequacy, which is a certain sense caused them to "act out." Now in some people, an inferiority complex as an enthusiastic may lie beneath the surface. However, others may be fully aware that they have a feature of themselves. They are not completely satisfied and trying to compensate.

When creating dark psychology as an outgrowth of internal mental ideas compared to Freudian psychoanalysis concepts, it may be simpler to assume. That human beings usually act with conscious, deliberate motivations instead of being consciously or unconsciously inspired by sexual urges, such as the well-studied complex of Oedipus (the desire for a man to kill his father and sleep). To truly comprehend the historical growth of dark psychology as a research field, it is crucial to realize that individual psychology's philosophy requires non-completely aware motives to explain why human beings tend to act in such a cruel fashion. Even so, the theory of dark psychology supposes that humans are capable of a dark universe, engaging in harmful actions that have no purpose at all.

The research and therapy of psychological disorders have been around as a field of study since the Ancient Egyptians. We have more data from the Greek period, partly because we are closer to the Greek philosophy period in time than we are from the Egyptians. This group just seems to reach the concept of pathology with a fascinating avidity. The research of what we term pathological psychology today existed in the 18th and 19th centuries and earlier in asylum and hospices that diagnosed people and women with rare mental disorders, but the discipline as we now know it dates from the 20th century.

Indeed, in the 19th century, trepanation, exorcism, and being burnt on the stakes as a witch were the standard remedies for pathological mental conditions. Trepanation relates to drilling a hole in the brain to expel malignant spirits from their grip over the head. It is claimed by others to be the earliest surgical technique we have historical evidence. Trepanation was already performed in the 19th century. Today, there are proponents of the procedure, though their appeals usually fell on deaf ears.

Exorcism also looks at how society viewed odd habits and emotions in the current age. Indeed, many practices that we consider to fall inside the normal range today have been considered mental diseases up till the early 1980s. Exorcism, although maybe less brutal than trepanation, represented the perspective that an evil force or demon inhabited the individual who possessed the weird thoughts and actions. All this has been a transmission from the individual's malevolent encouragement to anything else, whether something else was an informant of evil or an agent of evil.

One line of thinking recognizes Satan as the manifestation of human potential to act in a manner "strange" or, more accurately, evil or cruel. It is hard to say whether their ideas of ghouls, demons, values, or even of Satan himself embody that people beings were produced to commit acts of possession. They could be better described as stories intended to fool children or teach them valuable life lessons of good and evil. Of course, exorcisms are still happening today; individuals who assume evil acts come from ownership.

If you believe that the evil committed by human beings comes from a source outside the human being, then the dark psychological theory because it currently stands may be somewhat contrary to what you believe. However, a locally crucial in dark psychology is the idea that humans can behave without purpose in a remarkably violent and cruel manner, only as an augmentation of something obscure that dwells inside us. It is up to you to ascribe this type of conduct to Satan as a component of your religious views.

Of course, 19th-century and later abnormal psychologists did not fully recognize this idea of an independent factor for the conditions they were seeing. So treatments such as trepanation or exorcism would've been disturbing or at least pointless to them. As we commented on earlier, scientists shifted away towards the dogmatic beliefs that dominated their careers, ideologies that mostly had more to do with theology than with the professions' empirical compendia. There is nothing intrinsically inconsistent with religious belief, of course. Still, a practitioner who is inexperienced with human anatomy if he is not permitted to examine q cadaver is probably to follow a religion that is not advantageous to him (or herself) or you.

Abnormal psychologists started to question why humans were inspired to behave abnormally. The Devil or the Demons were not entirely acceptable responses. Most of these research groups in psychological disorders were psychiatrists and psychoanalysts who undertook detailed studies of these subjects based on a new, more free understanding of health matters. Though the word dark psychology did not emerge until later in the mid-twentieth century, narcissists, sociopaths, and those who we might identify today as possessing mental illnesses were conducted already throughout the 19th-century studies.

Abnormal psychology of that time would have followed the trend of what we now understand as Freudian psychoanalysis, with Alfred Adler's writings representing one of Freudian's first significant departures. Although Adler is a virtually unknown figure today, his biographies from the generations 1912-1914 provided the basis of many concepts that permeate today's psychological field. His writings were translated into English in 1925. And his personality beliefs and where they derive from predominate in advance psychotherapy and psychoanalysis.

Adler focused on resignation, compensation, and over-compensation as the 3 external factors that shaped personality development. His theories parallel those of another essential psychologist, Abraham Maslow, who acknowledged Alder's influence on his work. Although Adler himself didn't even write about "dark psychology," his theories helped shape this topic's development as a departure from pre-existing psychoanalytical theories.

The analysis of dark psychology can be new. Still, it reflects a spectrum of habits that have been associated with individuals from the very start. The dark area of psychology provides the illusion of a transient research domain. The word and the principles connected with it are more widely available to the people. This has turned dark psychological into a topic that remains beyond the radar of those who may be victims of perpetrators exploiting their resources to damage impact.

Chapter 6. Advanced Techniques to Manipulate Human Psychology

S ources tell us that it is concealment—hiding in the shadows, knowing when to strike. It is also a false front, hiding true intentions. When we are talking about this level of deception, we are talking about hiding aggression. When we take, there is a certain level of aggressive behavior that happens. A small part of manipulation is hiding that aggressive behavior so that the victim sees only good nature.

This is accomplished in various ways and means, one being knowledge. When we allow another to know us, we display vulnerability along with strengths. The experience of these personality traits can give the manipulator the ability to maneuver around without any alarms going off.

- The effectiveness of manipulating those strengths and vulnerabilities arrives when the dark practitioner knows what is vulnerable and inspires pride.

A reoccurring ideology that drives us to war takes into consideration that the action is more negative than positive. We want to avoid it. The manipulation process sees pride in all of us and plays to that pride. It is our strength. For example, when used to drive an army to slaughter others, the intention of our satisfaction has been manipulated to enforce the agendas of others.

- Often, the practitioners of dark psychology use aggression and fear to drive us. The less dark side still falls into the category of knowing what weakness is. That weakness leaves the individual open to control.

How the manipulator uses that control determines the severity of manipulation. There are positive versions of manipulating others, like convincing someone that they are not doing well and needing help. We, however, are looking at the darker side of this. The manipulator uses their control skills to get what they want—and the cost does not apply.

- There are many ways to move another into a place of being controlled. From the positive to the negative, psychological manipulators utilize all tactics.

When positive reinforcement is used, the charm is displayed. A forced smile or laughter can trigger laughter in all of us. As when we were infants, we copy what we see. When we see tears, we want them to stop. When we see a smile, we find ourselves smiling as well. Using positive reinforcement, the manipulator can shower money, charm, and gifts to get us to feel something. The usage of these things allows control of us on an instinctual level. We follow those who tell us what we want to hear.

- Psychological manipulation can also implement negative reinforcement. This is a form of deflection—the substitution of one thing for another.

Often, we have things we need or have to do, and we do not want to do them. The psychological manipulation of negative reinforcement uses that power of negativity to lure the subject from their original need, pushing them toward something they want to be done instead. The long game, a slow play of putting tasks into another's life and then controlling those tasks so that the manipulator can get what they want, is an extraordinarily useful and subdued tactic. Sometimes only partial reinforcement is required to gain control. We are talking about elevating the fear or doubt regarding the tasks needed to be done. The partial is the extended play. It knows that in the end, the victim will lose. It knows that by planting small seeds now, victory will eventually happen. It knows that we all have our weaknesses and that by planting even a tiny seed, we can take someone to that weakness. An individual trying to work toward something they already were shaky on or had doubts about will listen to the lie and flow with that idea, and use it to their destruction.

- The partial manipulator only needs to put the thought in mind, knowing the weakness is already there, and utilizing it will take their prey to a destructive end.

Psychological manipulators flat, outright punish. From an actual physical lashing to the victim's passive-aggressive playing, punishment is beneficial when one wants to control another.

- We skulk and cry and yell and nag and go completely silent. This is the blackmail of the manipulator. It inspires guilt in us. That "wanting to be the better person" rises to the front, and we do what the manipulator wants. When the manipulator sets free the crocodile tears, we have no idea if they are real or not. The degree of crying is not up to us to determine. Only the manipulator knows if the tears are legitimate or not. In this case, the trap is often sprung from the victim's side. They walk up to the hurt individual to help, only to find that the manipulator is just lying in wait to strike.

- One extreme version of manipulation is violence.

Violence triggers something inside us. We often do anything to avoid it. The manipulator knows that power strategically applied can make us go into a state of avoidance. There incites the control, physical violence can have mental scarring, and the manipulator causes the scarring. It places power in tactical places to get the result they want.

Some would say this is the darkest of the dark. Taken to the individual, this can mentally damage them for an extended period, if not permanently. Placed on a world stage, it can lead up to the physical conflict of genocide.

- Mostly, it is about gain. Manipulators of the dark want to gain something. When we speak about improvement, we are talking about power and influence, control and manipulation over others. The trophy is up to the individual. This can be everything as to gaining affections, to money, and even to life itself.

It is about gaining for their reasons and gratifications. The taking of others and making the power and control their own. Selfishness to the extreme. The mind of the dark practitioner sees the ultimate win as the gain over others. They have power. Superiority is the power over another, and taking of someone else's power makes them feel superior. This is a tremendous driving force behind the manipulator. Often, in the case of immature individuals driving manipulations toward superiority, any is pushed aside for just the feeling of being superior. In relationships, it is about control. The manipulation of power can put one in control. Although we have looked at the vampire and energy role, we know who has control.

This feeling of control can be overwhelming to the mental state of the dark. Almost drug-like, it is a feeling of emotion that is more logical. Management is one of the most straightforward manipulation tactics to achieve with only logic to guide. It drives not only the victim but the manipulator as well. Psychological manipulation can also be about self-esteem. The self of the manipulator is always in question. This is one of the reasons they manipulate, to define themselves. How easily they can manage, another can tell the dark that they are better than others. That weakness and strength can be measured in the tactical playing field of the hustle.

- The dark psychological manipulator is bored most of the time, more than most. The psychological manipulator will often use manipulation to determine the validity of feelings and emotions.

This boils down to that manipulation applied in relations with others helps the manipulator regulate reactions to validate or not validate their own emotions. The manipulator measures the self and their self-esteem by how others handle their self-questioning. This happens when the practitioner does not have a grasp on what emotions are. They look at their feelings as invalid and manipulate the situation in such a way as to validate them. We are stuck with ourselves, and we cannot get away. Psychological manipulators validate or invalidate themselves by the tactical controlling of others. It is an exciting way of viewing life, although we all idolize one form of manipulation.

- **The con aspect.** One common form of manipulation is the convincing of another to make their money's yours. This is a hidden agenda of the criminal. This form of mental manipulation preys mostly on the elderly and the rich. However, we all can fall into this form of manipulation. We choose to spend on, and we do not respond to a state of psychological manipulation.

Something happens when the buck is passed over, we go from manipulation into action, and something drives us. It is within us, and it is outside forces that drive. What causes this drive and the drive itself is called Persuasion.

The manipulation process in dark psychology usually is not a single move. It is a complex series of actions, often with the outcome only known by the manipulator. The motivations of manipulators are as convoluted as human nature.

Chapter 7. Mind Control

M ind control is an aspect of manipulation that is similar to brainwashing. The main difference is that the individual might only want to control your mind at the moment. Maybe they want to get you to do something that will benefit them temporarily because they are opportunistic individuals. Since there is not much time to take over a person's mind when you are engaged in a simple conversation, there are some very detailed techniques that a manipulator will use to attempt to gain control of your mind. As you explore these techniques, you will also learn how to combat each of them. The stronger your reason is, the better you will ward off the people trying to harm you.

Compensating for Lack of Physical Prowess

Someone might try to control your mind because you secretly intimate them. Because someone does not appear physically threatening, a manipulator will be quick to move forward with mind control by seeing how much they can change your thoughts. The mind control gives them the same type of satisfaction they would receive if they were physically controlling you. Because the latter is a lot more prominent, the idea of controlling your mind is also a lot more appealing. You will find that manipulators are very discreet about this.

They might remark on how strong or tough you are, building you up based on your physical characteristics. Even a simple comment about you being tall can be enough to let you think that they respect you because you have more physical prowess than they do—this is what they want you to think. Instead of backing down, which you will think they are doing, they make you more vulnerable by making you comfortable.

When you believe that someone sees powerful traits in you, you will be less likely to assume that they have bad intentions. Surely because they appear to respect you, they won't deceive you, right? Always make sure that you remind yourself anyone can fool you at any time. It is hard to keep track of everyone's true intentions, especially when they have mastered the art of mind control.

What You Can Do: Remain firm in your core beliefs. Even if you believe that the individual respects you and what you stand for, always remind yourself of what you hold dear to your heart. Staying true to who you give you little reason to change your opinions on a whim. Remind yourself that the person trying to control your mind is very insecure.

Using Hand Placement as a Decoy

Have you ever noticed that people normally place their fingers on their heads when thinking very hard? In moments of concentration, you have probably done the same thing. This is a subconscious mind control technique that is often used by manipulators. When they want you to rethink something, they might place their fingers on their head to coax you into doing the same. With the help of muscle memory, your brain will be receiving a message that it needs to think harder.

It is an interesting technique because it is so subtle. You surely would not notice it if you were not looking for it in the first place. As you become better at reading body language, you will become more aware of moments when the person you are talking to is merely using a decoy movement as an attempt to control you. Do your best to break the mirroring effect that typically happens during a conversation. Keep your arms in a neutral position by your side.

Manipulators get nervous. They probably get very nervous and will do the best they can to hide this from you. As soon as you notice their fingers move up to their head, imagine that they are nervous that they won't be able to pull off this attempt at mind control. Pride yourself in your ability to pick up on it before it affects you—this will keep you strong.

What You Can Do: In an attempt to break their cycle, you can make a comment that indirectly refers to them concentrating. Something like, "Oh, is that what you were thinking?" is a way to make manipulators second-guess their abilities. If you let them know from the start that you are not automatically going to agree with what they are saying, this will be your way of standing your ground.

Convincing You of Psychic Powers

The person who is manipulating you is not any more powerful than you—repeat this to yourself often. Even though many mind controllers are portrayed as psychic beings, this is not the case for most. A successful manipulator is usually just very good at picking up on your body language and context. There is nothing psychic about it, though it can feel that way at times.

Being misinformed that someone is psychic and can read your mind at any time is intimidating. These are your private thoughts, and you do not want anyone intruding upon them. The good news is that you never have to let this happen. You are still in control of your inner thoughts, and what you share with the world is always going to be your decision. Anyone who tries to force you or to coax you into sharing something you do not want to does not have your best interest at heart.

The mention of psychic abilities might come up as a joke. For example, the manipulator will joke around with you while mentioning that you don't need to say much because they already know what you are thinking. You can laugh this off, but you can also remain firm in believing that this isn't true. With the way you portray yourself, you can get them to think anything you want.

What You Can Do: Always be aware of your intention during every conversation. If you are presenting yourself in a certain way, the manipulative person will pick up on it. Try your hardest to practice standing neutrally and speaking neutrally. When you can master this concept, it will be a lot harder for them to read you.

Surrounding You with Other Manipulative People

This is an incredibly dangerous mind-control technique because it closely ties in with the idea behind brainwashing. The more people that you believe are on the same page about something will make you want to agree with them, too. If a manipulator can find other people who want to manipulate a vulnerable person, you might become an easy target for a bad situation. They will gang up on you in a way that is subtle yet effective. You do not have to put up with this. Knowing who you are as a person will protect you in many ways.

There will be times when a manipulator will only "scout" for like-minded individuals that believe in the point they are making. Unknowingly, they might recruit innocent bystanders to further lead you into thinking that you must agree with them. The people that also fall victim to these traps might be people you love and respect. This is why it might be tempting to give in and to just "go with the flow." It is what the manipulator wants you to think. They want others to know that it is easier to go with a mass opinion than form their own.

What You Can Do: Speak up when you disagree with something. This is difficult because you do not want to cause conflict or controversy, but it becomes necessary to protect yourself. A disagreement does not always have to turn into an argument. If you approach the situation maturely, you can simply speak your mind to get your point across without requiring validation. You can provide this for yourself. Remind yourself that it is not other people's opinions that matter most. Your view of yourself dictates your self-esteem.

Believing it Won't Happen to You

Because a mind controller works hard to use other people, you might assume that they would instead do this to strangers or bystanders. One of the most challenging realities to face is that these individuals are more likely to attempt the act of mind control on a loved one. This happens because the task seems a lot easier—they already know you well. Instead of having to figure out the things that get under your skin, they have an idea of what to say and how to persuade you. Realizing this can be very hurtful, especially when you have many trusts invested in the person.

"I would never do anything to hurt you" is a promise that is often broken by a manipulator. With mind control, they are directly going against that promise, even if it doesn't feel hurtful at the moment. When someone does not respect you for who you are, they will do anything to change you. Suggesting you should get something else to eat or that you should shop elsewhere for clothing are two simple examples of how manipulators can use their conviction to change you.

You might not believe that these little changes mean much, but when you add them up, they can completely transform who you are as a person. It is not a great feeling to realize that you no longer recognize who you are. As upsetting as it is, you have to work on rebuilding yourself and getting back to your roots. It is normal to feel betrayed because this is what the manipulator has done to you—betrayed your trust.

What You Can Do: Never let your naive thinking get in the way of your rational thinking. You are not immune to the mind control that goes on around you. Your strength does not necessarily protect you from the intentions of all manipulators. By keeping yourself humble, you will always be on alert for the red flags presented by those who wish to change your mind.

The Blank Stares of Intimidation

Making a statement to someone and receiving a blank stare in return is intimidating for many reasons. One of the most prominent is that you do not know what they are thinking. It scares you because you might not know what to say or do next. A manipulator will use this technique to control your mind after you have said something vulnerable or profound. This will make you second-guess if what you said was "wrong" or incorrect somehow. You will end up prioritizing their feelings over your own.

They might follow this instance up with a statement that seems wise or all-knowing. When you combine the two actions, you are sure to believe that they can read your mind or that they know something you don't know. Both possibilities are unsettling in their ways. When you feel a negative emotion, understand that this is what your manipulator wants you to feel. They want to catch you off-guard and make you question everything that you have confirmed in your reality. By slowly breaking you down and staring at you blankly, you will get the idea that you came to this conclusion independently. It becomes maddening when you do not realize what is happening to you.

Chapter 8. Mind Control Techniques

M ind control involves using influence and persuasion to change the behaviors and beliefs of someone. That someone might be the person themselves, or it might be someone else. Mind control has also been referred to as brainwashing, thought reform, coercive persuasion, mental control, and manipulation, just to name a few. Some people feel that everything is done by manipulation. But if that is true to be believed, then important points about manipulation will be lost. Influence is much better thought of as a mental continuum with two extremes. One side has respectful and ethical influences and works to improve the individual while showing respect for them and their basic human rights. The other side contains dark and destructive influences that work to remove that human rights from a person, such as independence, rational thought, and sometimes their real identity.

When thinking of mind control, it is better to see it use influence on other people to disrupt something in them, as their way of thinking or living. The influence works based on what makes people human, such as their behaviors, beliefs, and values. It can disrupt the very way they chose personal preferences or make critical decisions. Mind control is nothing more than using words and ideas to convince someone to say or do something they might never have thought of saying or doing on their own.

There are scientifically proven methods that can be used to influence other people. Mind control has nothing to do with fakery, ancient arts, or even magical powers. Real mind control is the basis of a word that many people hate to hear. That word is marketing. Many people hate to hear that word because of the negative connotations associated with it. When people hear "marketing," they automatically assume that it refers to those ideas taught in business school. But the basis of marketing is not about deciding which part of the market to target or deciding which customers will likely buy this product. The basis of marketing is one very simple word. That word is "YES."

If a salesperson asks a regular customer to write a brief endorsement of the product they buy, they will hopefully say yes. If someone asks their significant other to take some of the business cards to pass out at work, they will hopefully say yes. If you write any blog and ask another blogger to provide a link to yours on their blog, they will hopefully say yes. When enough people say yes, the business or blog will begin to grow. With even more yesses, it will continue to grow and thrive. This is the very simple basis of marketing. Marketing is nothing more than using mind control to get other people to buy something or do something beneficial. And the techniques can easily be learned.

The first technique in mind control is to tell people what you want them to want. Never tell people to think it over or take some time. That is a definite mind control killer. People already have too much going on in their minds. When they are told to think something over, they will not. It will be forgotten, and then it will never happen. This has nothing to do with being stupid or lazy and everything to do with just being way too busy.

So the best strategy is to take the offensive and think for them. Everything must be explained in the beginning. Never assume that the other blogger will automatically understand the benefits of adding a link will be for them. Do not expect anyone to give a demonstration blindly. And merely asking for a testimonial, while it might garner an appositive response, probably will not garner a well-formed testimonial to the product. Instead, be prepared to explain the blog, show examples, and offer compelling reasons why this merger will benefit both parties. Have the demonstration laid out in great detail with notes on what to say when and visuals to go along with the letters, so all the other person has to do is present the information. Offer the customer a few testimonials that have already been received and ask them to choose one and personalize it a bit. Always be specific in explaining what is desired. Explain why it is desired. Show how this will work. Tell the person how to do it and why they should do it. If done correctly, it will feel exactly like one friend advising another friend on which is the best path to take. And the answer will be yes, simply because saying yes makes so much sense.

Think of the avalanche. Think of climbing all the way to the top of the highest mountain ever. Now, at the top, think of searching for the biggest, heaviest boulder on the mountain. Now, picture summoning up superhuman strength to push this boulder, dislodging it from the place it has rested for years and years. Once this boulder is loosened, it rolls easily over the edge of the cliff, crashing into thousands of other boulders on its way down the mountain, taking half of the mountain with it in a beautiful cascade of rocks and dirt. Imagine sitting there, smiling cheerfully at the avalanche that was just created.

Marketing and mind control are very like creating an avalanche. Getting the first person to answer yes might be difficult. But each subsequent yes will be easier. Always start at the top, never the bottom. Starting at the top is more complicated. It is more likely to come with more negative responses than positive responses in the beginning. But starting at the top also yields a much greater reward when the avalanche does begin. And the results will be far greater than beginning at the bottom of the mountain. Yes, the small rock is easier to push over. Then it can be built upon by pushing over another small rock, then another. This way can work, but it will take much longer than being successful at the top. No one ever went fishing for the smallest fish in the pond or auditioned for the secondary role just to be safe. Everyone wants that top prize. Do not be afraid to go for it.

On the other hand, never ask for the whole boulder the first time. Ask for part of it. This may seem directly contradictory, but it is not. Always start with a small piece. Make the beginning easier for everyone to see. Let other people use their insight to see the result. When the first bit goes well, then gradually ask for more and more and more.

Think of writing a guest spot for someone else who has their own blog. By sending in the entire manuscript first, there is a greater risk of rejection. Begin small. Send them a paragraph or two discussing them with the idea. Then outline the idea and send that in an email. Then write the complete draft you would like them to use and send it along. When asking a customer for a testimonial, start by asking for a few lines in an email. Then ask the customer to expand those few lines into a testimonial covering at least half a typed page. The customer will soon be ready for an hour-long webcast extolling the product's virtues and your great customer service skills.

Everything must have a deadline that exists. The important word here is the word 'real.' Everyone has heard the salesperson who said to decide right away because the deal might not be available later or another customer was coming in, and they might get it. That is a total fabrication, and everyone knows it to be true. There are no impending other customers, and the deal is not going to disappear. There is no real sense of urgency involved. But everyone does it. There are too many situations where people are given a fake deadline by someone who thinks it will instill a great sense of urgency for completing the task. It is not only totally not effective but completely unneeded. It is a simple matter to create true urgency. Only leave free things available for a finite amount of time. When asking customers for testimonials, be certain to mention the last possible day for it to be received to be able to be used. Some people will be unable to assist, but having people unable to participate is better than never beginning.

Always give before you receive it. And do not ever think that giving is fifty-fifty. Always give much more than is expected in return. Before asking for a testimonial from a satisfied customer, be sure to make numerous acts of exceptional customer service. Before asking a blog writer for a link, link theirs to yours many times. This is not about helping someone out so that they will help you. This is all about being so totally generous that the person who is asked for the favor cannot possibly say no. It might mean extra work, but that is how to influence other people.

Always stand up for something much bigger than average. Do not just write another blog on how to do something. Use a critical issue to take a stand and defend the stance with unbeatable logic and genuine passion. Do not just write a how-to manual. Choose a particular idea and sell people on it, using examples of other people with the same idea living the philosophy.

Never feel shame. This does not mean being extremely extroverted to the point of silliness or having a total lack of conscience in business dealings. In mind control, shamelessness refers to a full, complete belief that this course of action is the best possible course. Everyone will benefit greatly from it. This is about writing the best possible blog ever and believing that everyone needs to read it to improve their lives. It is about believing in a particular product so deeply that the feeling is that everyone will benefit from using it. Knowing deep inside that this belief is the correct belief ever and everyone should believe it.

Mind control uses the idea that someone's decisions and emotions can be controlled using psychological means. It uses negotiation or mental influence powers to ensure the outcome of the interaction is more favorable to one person over the other. This is what marketing is: convincing someone to do something particular or buy something in particular. Being able to control someone else's mind merely means understanding the power of human emotion and playing upon those emotions. It is easier to have a mental impact on people if there is a basic understanding of human emotions. Angry people will back down when the subject of their anger is not afraid. Angry people feed upon the fear of others.

Chapter 9. Influence People With Mind Control

A mind controller approaches the victim with the sole intent of cloning themselves, making the other person think like them. This is a complicated thing to do, so, to achieve it, one has to possess an inflated ego, lack doubts about themselves, and have a high sense of entitlement. All of us are susceptible to manipulation, and what matters is how much effect the mind control will have on us.

Psychologists studying mind control have found out that the entire process seems to adhere to a typical structure. This conclusion was made after a study was conducted on multiple marketing and networking companies which used mind control to persuade clients to purchase their products. One of the remarkable similarities is that all new members joining the companies underwent pre-planned training to recruit more people and convince potential customers to buy their products. The training sessions are meant to make the employees think like the company wants and use a mind twist to convince people.

Let us now look at the mind control process in detail:

Step 1: Understanding the target

Before anything else, the manipulator will seek to establish a bond or connection with their potential victim. Good intent, or friendship, will be the first step because it makes the victim lower all their social and psychological defenses. Once the controller gains the target's trust, they start reading them to devise the most effective method to invade them. The reading aims to tell whether their victim is susceptible to their manipulation. Just like any project manager, they do not like wasting time on a subject they suspect might outsmart them and lead to failure.

Multiple clues are used to scan the victim. They include vocal style, body language, social status, gender, emotional stability, etc. A person's traits can be used to decode the strength of their defenses. All this time, the manipulator will be asking themselves questions like, "Are you introvert or extrovert?" "Are you weakly?" "Are you emotional?" "Are you self-confident?" Humans give a lot of information about themselves when interacting with each other. This is something that the controller knows all too well. From these signs, they can quickly tell if the person is cooperating. They will look at body posture and immediately analyze the victim. Excess blinking might insinuate that a person is lying. Arms folded across the chest might show a lack of interest or insecurity. Taking enormous strides while walking might portray fear. As you can see, the body releases so much data at any given time that it is essential to be aware of the signs that you are giving out

When the attacker has collected enough data from the target, they now understand their interests, strengths, weaknesses, routines, and so on. Using this information, they can decide on an entry point, which will allow for easy and accurate manipulation. They also determine whether the target is worth the effort. If they see one as a favorable target, they move to the other step in the mind control process- unfreezing factual beliefs and values.

Step 2: Unfreezing Solid Beliefs and Values

All of us have some beliefs and values engraved deep within. Most of them are the principles that were instilled in us since childhood, and others have been acquired from experiences are we grow older. We rarely let go of them, but revise them as we proceed. Most of them make up our identities, so we do not like them being interfered with. If these principles are threatened, contradicted, or questioned at any point in time, our natural reaction is to defend them through all means possible. However, if a good-enough reason is given to us, so we voluntarily question them ourselves; we undergo a process known as "unfreezing."

Tons of reasons can lead us to unfreeze: a breakup, the death of a loved one, religious interference, getting evicted from our houses, to mention but a few. These situations force us to seek answers to complex cases, which goes as deep as questioning our sole beliefs and values. Take this, for example:

Way back when I am a teenager, we had some family friends who were solid Christians. It happens that my best friend, who was my exact age, came from this family. His name was Sam. Sam used to tell me about the Bible and its teachings, trying to convince me to accept salvation and live according to its instructions. I remember asking him why he was so insistent on this issue. He would respond that all problems were solvable with saving and that life was much more comfortable and happier. Fast-forward about fifteen years, Sam's mother was diagnosed with breast cancer. They tried all forms of treatment available at the time, but the cancer would grow back. One day, while talking to him about the issue, he looked at me with a pale face and said, "I think what they say about Christianity is not real!" Unsure about what he had just said, I asked him why he thought so. He responded that they had met tens of spiritual leaders for prayers, but his mother's cancer was only getting worse. What's worse, she would not live for more than a year.

Sad as Sam's story is, it makes us realize that some situations in life might force us to question the vital principles that we grow up with. In this case, my best friend had come to doubt the very same religion that he once felt had automatic solutions to all of life's problems. In the very same manner, a manipulator will dig deep into their victim's life to understand their vulnerabilities and exploit them fully. These people will say anything they think their targets would love to hear. Once the victim swallows the manipulator's comfort, there is a shift in power dynamics, and the target is now ready for the manipulation.

Step 3: Reprogramming the Mind

The mind control process seeks to separate the target from their initial beliefs and begin reprogramming their mind. The reprogramming is meant to install the manipulator's beliefs and values into the victim's mind. Apart from distancing the initial principles, the controller also tries their best to make them look wrong or harmful, or the cause of past mishaps in the victim's life. If the victim absorbs this reprogramming, their defense is lowered to zero, and they now become a robot that is ready to accept any operating system that is offered.

During the reprogramming phase, the attacker will ensure the victim has minimal contact with the outside world. They make everyone else appear insignificant to the victim because this raises their opportunity to deposit their malicious principles. This behavior is typical in cults, mostly crafted to sway their followers from mainstream human life. Some cults go as far as controlling their followers' food intake as a way of weakening them. The psychology behind this idea is that a weak person will always turn to the person they feel has the power to protect them or alleviate their suffering. The same happens in relationships, where one partner plays the controlling role. The victimized one has no choice but to adhere to the other. You might wonder why some people put up with violent partners. Still, so far, you must already understand that the problem is more profound than it appears. If you control a person's mind, you can control their lives.

Once the victim has been reprogrammed, the manipulator moves into the final phase of the mind control process known as "freezing."

Step 4: Freezing the New Beliefs and Values

Once the victim has been fed with contrasting principles by the offender, the offender applies tactics to cement the new beliefs into their brains. This is what psychologists call "freezing." The freezing bit is necessary because the controller is aware of the person's original ideas that might clash with their initial ones. As such, they need to force the victim to choose their malicious principles over their old ones. To do this, they might apply any of the following methods.

One of the methods is using the reward/punishment approach. When the victim acts according to the manipulator's demands, they are rewarded. Hopefully, you see the similarity between the freezing process and dog training. The dog is given treats when it follows the trainer's instructions. The trainer aims at solidifying the new skill in the dog by rewarding it. In the future, if the dog is instructed to do the same thing, it will not hesitate since it has been made to think that obeying the command is useful and attracts a reward. The same applies to mind control; when the victim follows, they are made to feel that what they did was right and deserves a reward.

Punishments are the second most-applied approach in the freezing process. If the victim deviates from the controller's commands, they are punished. If we go back to a cult scenario, they usually have defined punishments for violations of terms. During the Holocaust, for instance, any Germans who failed to hail Hitler were punished through imprisonment or death. In the same way, any German who was suspected of protecting the Jews was shot. Hitler understood that by punishing anyone who went against his rules, he would force every German to help him attain his ethnic cleansing objective. The psychological trick used in these situations is that the victim is made to see punishment as justice being served for breaking the rules.

Mind controllers' final method to solidify their manipulation is to transform their victims into their agents. Better put, once the controller feels that the victim's pseudo personality has materialized, they use them to distribute their worldviews. We said that the mind controller's list is to create a replica of themselves in the other person. Therefore, once the controlling process is complete, the victim starts living like the attacker without realizing it. Depending on the manipulation's nature, the victim might also be used to recruit more victims into the oppressor's way of thinking and living. This is especially true in the context of marketing and networking. From this explanation, we can readily tell why a wife is likely to be violent towards the kids if the husband is violent. The kids are also expected to be violent towards each other or their friends. The process of mind control is slow, but once it solidifies, it can result in devastating effects.

Chapter 10. Dark Persuasion

Whenever folks try to provide meaning to the notion of demeanor, their responses always come in various forms. Even though some could put their thoughts on the ads and advertisements which are everywhere in contemporary society, advocating you to patronize a specific product or service over the other others' heads fall back into the politicians who attempt to modify the minds of Republicans simply to get yet another vote in the polls. Both instances are right since they are messages targeted at altering the understanding of this topic. The purpose of diversion between ordinary persuasion and dim persuasion is the dark persuasion doesn't necessarily have a moral rationale.

Even though a standard persuader might attempt to convince someone for this individual's own great, a dim persuader does so together with motives that are not always great for another individual. They try to obtain a total grasp of the individual they would like to convince and take pains to do this since they understand the greatest motivation.

While persuasion consistently has ethical consequences, a dim persuader doesn't concern themselves with those consequences. In reality, they are mindful of these, but decide to put their eyes on their goal (s) rather than persuasion as a mental phenomenon in an individual's regular life. It's either that you're the person attempting to convince someone else or you're being persuaded. What makes the distinction between dark and ordinary is that the motivation for this. In mass media, politics, legal and advertising conclusions, persuasion comes to play all of the time. The results of instructing it in such areas are set utilizing persuasion to determine the topic of influence.

There are a few clear and crucial differences between behavioral and other brain control varieties, like brainwashing and hypnosis. Even though these two demands that the topic should be isolated from modifying their thoughts and individuality, persuasion doesn't require isolation. To be able to reach the target, manipulation is utilized on a single individual. Although persuasion may also be performed on a single topic to make them change their thoughts, there's also a chance of using it on a vast scale to alter the heads of an entire group or a whole society.

Because of this, persuasion is a much better mind control procedure and maybe more harmful since it can alter the minds of lots of people at precisely the same time rather than the head of only one individual at one time. Many people produce the error of believing that they have immunity to the consequences of persuasion because they think that they will always have the ability to observe every sales pitch that comes in their way.

They think they'll always have the ability to use logic to grasp what's happening and find a logical decision for this. As a result of how people aren't ever likely to fall for whatever they hear, this might be accurate if they utilize logic. It's likewise feasible to steer clear of persuasion since the debate doesn't augur nicely with the individual's beliefs, whatever the strength of this debate. Some individuals understand how to use clear messages to inspire people to market the industry's newest gadgets or goods. This information action is quite delicate, so the topic won't always recognize it; therefore, it's going to be rather difficult for them to continually have the ability to decide the information they will get.

Every time is said, it's extremely probable that you think about it in a terrible light. That is because it is inclined to automatically consider a conman or salesman who's always attempting to make them modify their view, and that will finally push them till this shift is reached. While black persuasion is notable in earnings and conning clinics, also, there are ways that persuasion may be used permanently, such as in diplomatic relationships between global bodies or at public service attempts. The difference only lies in the method by which in which the practice of persuasion is attracted to perform.

Dark Persuasion Methods

When an individual is prepared to modify the head of the topic by devoting them to do anything against their first frame of mind, the persuader will get some nicely laid out methods to help them reach their targets. Every day that passes, the goal will face various kinds of persuasion. Food manufacturers aim to receive their goal to test the recipes that are new or have them adhere to the earlier ones, even while studios may flaunt their most recent blockbuster films about the faces of the aims. In any situation may be whatever merchandise they're promoting, their principal intent is to generate more revenue, and that's the reason they're attempting to convince you. They couldn't care less about how this may affect you, and that is why they need to be quite careful and proficient in the art of subtle persuasion to make sure they don't deceive you off or make you plump.

As there are also lots of different brands attempting to convince you, they need to locate an exceptional approach to impress their perspectives on you. As a result of the effect of info on a vast selection of individuals, the methods used in it's been a topic of research for several decades, dating back to early times. That is because the influence is a really helpful instrument in controlling a large assortment of individuals. Beginning in the early 20th century, the proper analysis of those techniques started to grow. Bear in mind that the objective of attempting to convince people would be to push a compelling debate in an audience and have the positive.

They'll then internalize this information and embrace it as their fresh mindset or even means of life. Because of this, there's a great need to find very prosperous persuasion methods. Three dark persuasion methods are of fantastic value through recent years. We will go over those three:

Create a Need

This is only one of the most profitable methods of obtaining an individual to change their perspective or lifestyle. The individual hoping to convince a goal will create demand or concentrate on a demand that the topic already has. If that is achieved suitably, it's the capacity of enticing a fantastic deal to your goal. This signifies that to become prosperous, the persuader should interest in the demands that are far more significant to the goal.

This could be their requirement to fulfill their fantasies of fostering their self-esteem. It might also function as a desire for love, food, or shelter. This method will work out nicely since there's not anyway the topic isn't likely to require one or more of these items or need of anything at all for that matter. As there's not always, the goal is not likely to get dreams and ambitions. The persuader will probably simply find strategies to produce the sufferer understand how they can easily help the sufferer attain those dreams. The persuader can also tell their goal the goal will probably recognize their visions if they make certain adjustments to their faith or outlook.

As stated by the persuader, doing this will provide the target with a greater prospect of attaining success. For example, a young guy who wishes to get romantic with a woman may inform her that he'll help her boost her grades and eventually make her parents happy by obtaining a. Still, only when she's friends with his or her although this woman may believe she has finally discovered the salvation she desires, the simple truth is that the young guy is not very curious about how she plays in college. Her teenagers are just a lure for obtaining access to sexual activity.

Appealing to Social Needs

Another technique the persuader may utilize is identifying the goal of social demands. Even though this might not yield as many outcomes and the goal's main requirements will, it's still a powerful instrument in the hands of the persuader. Some are naturally attracted to audiences and want to be desired. They always wish for certain things, not because they want them, but because it includes certain prestige, making them feel like they belong to a bigger course. The idea of appealing to your target's societal needs is what's accessible through several TV advertisements where audiences are invited to purchase a product so they won't be "left behind." When they could recognize and allure to the societal needs of their goal, the outcome is that they can achieve a new field of the goal's interest.

Making Use of Loaded Words and Images

When an individual is hoping to convince someone else, they need to be cautious with their selection of words because words could make all of the difference. When there are many means to say something, one way of stating it might be more potent than another. When it's related to persuasion, among the essential things is understanding how to say the ideal thing at the ideal moment. Words are the most effective tools in communicating and understanding the perfect call-to-action phrases.

Dark persuasion is just one of the most effective dim psychology theories, but regrettably, it's always overlooked and suppressed. This might be because, unlike many different head control procedures, persuasion renders the goal using a selection. At another mind control procedure, the aim is forced to enter.

Occasionally, this is achieved by placing them into isolation to ensure, in conclusion, they don't have any say in the procedure results. Regarding persuasion, the chips have been laid bare (though with the ulterior purpose in dim persuasion), so the goal is made to make the choice they think will fit them best.

Conclusion

After looking at the different types of persuasion and what they all mean, you may see why dark persuasion is such a bad thing and can be harmful to the victim. Recognizing the different techniques that the manipulator may use can make it easier to understand when used on you.

So, how exactly is a dark persuader able to use this idea to carry out their wishes? There are a few different types of tactics that a dark manipulator is going to use. Still, some of the most common options include:

The Long Con

The first method that we are going to look at is the Long Con. This method is kind of slow and drawn out, but it can be effective because it takes so long, and it is hard to recognize or pinpoint when something went wrong. One of the main reasons that some people can resist persuasion is that they feel that they are being pressured by the other person, making them back off. If they feel that there is a lack of rapport or trust with the person trying to persuade them, they will steer clear. The Long Con is effective because they can overcome these main problems and give the persuader precisely what they want.

The Long Con will involve the dark persuader to take their time, working to earn their victim's trust. They will take some time to befriend the victim and make sure that their victims trust and like them. The persuader will achieve this with artificial rapport building, which sometimes seems excessive, and other techniques will help increase the comfort levels between the persuader and their victim.

As soon as the persuader sees that the victim is adequately readied psychologically, the persuader will begin their attempts. They may start with some insincere positive persuasion. The persuader will lead their victim to choose or do some activities that will benefit the persuader. This is going to serve the persuader in two ways. First, the victim starts to become used to persuasion by that persuader. The second is that the victim will start making that mental association between a positive outcome and the persuasion.

The Long Con will take a long period to complete because the persuader doesn't want to make it too obvious what they are doing. An example of this is a victim who is a recently widowed lady who is vulnerable because of her age and from their grief. After her loss, a man starts to befriend her. This man may be someone she knows from church or even a relative. He starts to spend more time with her, showing immense kindness and patience, and it doesn't take too long for her guard to drop when he comes around.

Then this man starts to carry out some smaller acts of positive persuasion that we talked about before. He may advise her of a better bank account to use or a better way to reduce any monthly bills. The victim will appreciate these efforts and the fact that the man is trying to help her, and she takes the advice.

Over some time, the man then tries to use some dark persuasion. He may try to persuade her to let him invest some of her money. She obliges because of the positive persuasion that was used in the past. Of course, the man is going to work to take everything he can get from her. If the manipulator is skilled enough, she may feel that he actually tried to help her, but the money is lost because he just ran into some bad luck with the investment. This is how far dark persuasion can go.

Graduality

Often when we hear about acts of dark persuasion, it seems impossible and unbelievable. They fail to realize that this dark persuasion isn't ever going to be a big or a sudden request that comes out of nowhere. Dark persuasion is more like a staircase. The dark persuader will never ask the victim to do something big and dramatic the first time they meet. Instead, they will have the victim take one step at a time.

When the manipulator has the target only go one step at a time, the whole process seems like less of a big deal. Before the victim knows it, they have already gone a long way down, and the persuader isn't likely to let them leave or come back up again.

Let's take an example of how this process is going to look in real life. Let's say that there is a criminal who wanted to make it so that someone else committed the crimes for them. Gang bosses, cult leaders, and even Charles Manson did this same thing.

This criminal wouldn't dream of beginning the process by asking their victim to murder for them. This would send out a red flag, and no one in their right minds would willingly go out and kill for someone they barely know. Instead, the criminal would start by having the victim do something small, like a petty crime, or simply hiding a weapon for them. Something that isn't that big of a deal for the victim, at least in comparison.

Over time, the acts that the manipulator can persuade their victim to do will become more severe. And since they did the smaller crimes, the persuader now has the unseen leverage of holding some of those smaller misdeeds over the victim, kind of like for blackmail. Before the victim knows it, they are going to feel like they are in too deep. They will then be persuaded to carry out some of the most shocking crimes. And often, by this point, they will do it because they feel like they have no other choice.

Dark persuaders will be experts at using this graduality to help increase the severity of their persuasion over time. They know that no victim would be willing to jump the canyon or do the big crime or misdeed right away. So, the persuader works to build a bridge to get there. By the time the victim sees how far they are, it is too late to turn back.

Masking the True Intentions

There are different methods that a persuader can use dark psychology to get the things that they want. Disguising their true desires is very important for them to be successful. The best persuaders can use this approach in various ways. Still, the method they choose is often going to depend on the victim and the situation.

One principle used by a persuader is that many people will have a difficult time refusing two requests when they happen in a row. Let's say that the persuader wants to get $200 from the victim, but they do not intend to repay the money. The persuader may begin by saying that they need a loan for the amount of $1000. They may go into some details about the consequences to themselves if the persuader doesn't come up with that kind of money sometime soon.

The victim may feel guilt or compassion for the persuader, and they want to help. But $1000 is a lot of money, more than the victim can lend. From here, the persuader is going to lessen their request from $1000 down to $200, the amount that they wanted from the beginning. Of course, there is some emotional reason for needing the money. The victim feels like it is impossible to refuse this second request. They want to help out the persuader, and they feel bad for not giving in to the initial request when they were asked. In the end, the persuader gets the $200 they originally wanted, and the victim is not going to know what has taken place.

Another type of technique that the persuader can use is known as reverse psychology. This can also help to mask true intentions during the persuasion. Some people have a personality that is known as a boomerang. This means that they will refuse to go in the direction they are thrown away and instead will veer off into different directions.

If the persuader knows someone more of a boomerang type, they can identify a key weakness. For example, let's say that a persuader has a friend attempting to win over some girl they like. The persuader knows that the friend will use and then hurt that girl. The girl is currently torn between a malicious friend and an innocent third party. The persuader may try to steer the girl in the direction of the guy who is a good choice, knowing that she will go against this and end up going with the harmful friend.

Leading Questions

Another method of dark persuasion that can be used is known as leading questions. If you have ever had an encounter with a skilled salesman, verbal persuasion can be really impactful when deployed in careful and calibrated ways. One of the most powerful techniques that can be used verbally is leading questions.

These leading questions will be any questions intended to trigger a specific response out of the victim. The persuader may ask the target something like, "how bad do you think those people are?" This question will imply that the people the persuader is asking about are bad to some extent. They could have chosen to ask a non-leading question, such as "how do you feel about those people?"

Dark persuaders are masters at using leading questions in a way that is hard to catch. If the victim ever begins to feel that they are being led, they will resist, and it is hard to lead them or persuade them. If a persuader ever senses that their victim starts to catch what is happening, they will quit using that one and switch over to another. They may come back to that tactic, but only when the victim has quieted down a bit and is more influenceable again.

The Law of State Transference

The state is a concept that will take a look at the general mood someone is in. If someone is aligned with their deeds, words, and thoughts, this is an example of a healthy and harmonious state. The law of state transference will involve the concept of someone who holds the balance of power in a situation and can then transfer their emotional state onto the other person they interact with. This can be a potent tool for the dark persuader to use against their victim.

Initially, the influencer will force their state to match the state that their target naturally has. If the target is sad and talks slowly, the influencer will make their state follow this format. The point of this is to create a deep rapport with the target.

After we get to this state match, the influencer will alter their state subtly and see if they have some compliance for the victim. Perhaps they will choose to speed up their voice to see if the victim will speed up as well. Once the victim starts to show these signs of compliance, the influencer is at the hook point.